Breaking Up With The Moon

poems by

Jennifer Lighty

Finishing Line Press
Georgetown, Kentucky

Breaking Up With The Moon

Copyright © 2016 by Jennifer Lighty
ISBN 978-1-944251-50-5 First Edition
All rights reserved under International and Pan-American Copyright Conventions.
No part of this book may be reproduced in any manner whatsoever without written permission from the publisher, except in the case of brief quotations embodied in critical articles and reviews.

ACKNOWLEDGMENTS

"Broken Water" first appeared in *Where Beach Meets Ocean: The Anthology of The Block Island Poetry Project*
"Breathing Again after a Long Time Underwater" was first published in *Bamboo Ridge*.
"Confessional" first appeared in *Thrush Poetry Journal*.
"That Which There Are No Words For," "Shaping the Dark," and "The Door," appeared first in *The Beloit Poetry Journal*.
"In Ceremony" was first published in *Room*.

Gratitude to Fran Quinn, Lisa Starr, John Rosenwald, Ekiwah Adler Belendez, Timothy Liu, Katie Rauk, Vernon Fowlkes and Jim Elsaesser for their help with these poems and to the two communities- The Block Island Poetry Project and The Great Mother Conference-who held me as I dissolved inside my chrysalis, supporting me with tenderness as my wings dried and my words caught air and flew.

Editor: Christen Kincaid

Cover Art: Steven Lighty

Author Photo: T. Finn Photography

Cover Design: Elizabeth Maines

Printed in the USA on acid-free paper.
Order online: www.finishinglinepress.com
also available on amazon.com

Author inquiries and mail orders:
Finishing Line Press
P. O. Box 1626
Georgetown, Kentucky 40324
U. S. A.

Table of Contents

Crossing The Field 1
Halfway Up The Mountain 2
The Door 4
Self Portrait 5
Ghost Moon Lullaby 6
Shaping The Dark 7
How To See Light With Your Eyes Closed 8
Broken Water 9
Parting The Sea 10
Left Without Words 12
The Full Moon's Shadow 13
Mirror, Mirror 14
What The Man In The Moon Has To Say 15
Breaking Up With The Moon 16
Poem To Our Third Body 18
Blessed Without Words 19
Broken Chains 21
In Ceremony 22
Confessional 23
Breathing Again After A Long Time Underwater ... 24
That Which There Are No Words For 26
Where The Sky Is Born 28

We are going to the moon—that is not very far.
Man has so much farther to go within himself.
—Anaïs Nin

I'm sick of my own romanticism!
—Anaïs Nin

Crossing the Field

I move on my breath
through a veil of milkweed
toward the deer on the far side of the field.

A chorus of unseen insects
fills in my footsteps, swelling
beyond hard shells

into the soft places of my body
I hide with solitude, saying to myself
I am not lonely.

The air shimmers with instinct.
With the doe's musk
and the buck's desire to mate.

The doe looks down as if
I don't exist, but the buck holds my gaze.

Antlers pierce the sun,
showering the field with ancient light.

I offer my palms to the milkweed.
My breath lifts the white filaments,
scatters seeds to the invisible.

So close   I can almost touch them.
The soft places of my body
open to their gaze. I know now

what I want: to desire like that,
defiant in daylight, sharp
against the sky's blue edges.

Halfway up the Mountain

Thousands of miles from home
without a reason I could name.
So high I struggled to breathe
and had to hand my pack to the boy
when he offered, flitting between
his father Eduardo and me like a sparrow.

I wanted to give up,
head back down, but the boy,
too small to carry me on his back,
was already heartbroken. Pain
cleaving my skull bones, I kept climbing,
fragile like a newborn
scanning the sky for her mother
who sees only the sun.

Light trapped in layers of mica glowed
as if the mountain was asking me to
peel it back in layers until its core was exposed.

When we reached a small plateau
where an old man sat on the ground
blocking the open door
of a stone hut without windows,
Eduardo asked me for the bag of coca leaves
he'd told me to buy at the market,
gave it to the old man who did not thank us.

A donkey staked just beyond his reach
brayed like a child for its mother,
hung its head when we turned
and kept climbing toward the village in the clouds
where six of us would sleep that night
in one room without windows.

When we were more than halfway up the mountain,
Eduardo said to me, "That was my father,"
as if it was normal to live that alone.

All night I wanted to run back down to see
if the old man let the donkey in when it
brayed in the dark, if he stroked its long ears,
held his cheek   to the soft fur covering its jawbone.

I didn't understand then why
I wanted so much to carry the old man with us,
why I was awake all night
while the others slept,
willing the morning to come
so I could walk out   alone on the mountain.

The Door

If we leave our front door open even
a crack, the dog comes in. *A fuera—out—*
I groan from my bed,
where I'm waiting out the sun
with a book of poems in which a woman
walks naked to a well and pulls a rope
like a serpent's tail
                out of the dark earth.

When she pours the cold water
over her skin, drops cling and glisten.
I sweat. Scratch fleabites. Cringe
when my roommate yells
with the necessary force to send the dog
out the door.

The dog is pregnant,
looking for a place to give birth.
The guys from the bar next door call her *Chaparrita*.
I'm told it's an endearment for short, chubby females.
They claim she's theirs,
though I don't know what that means,
here, or in any other country.
Yesterday I watched her gnaw
plastic bottles they threw in the street.

Every time she sneaks back in
she looks at us like this time
we'll realize we love her.

At sunset   the bar opens.
We lock the door.

Self Portrait

At night, the silver lamé curtain over the bar door
sparkles like champagne or phosphorescence. By day,
it's a different story. Girls crouch on plastic crates,
nursing babies in the six inches of shade cast by the bar roof.
They are young enough to be my daughters, but they look older.
When I haul my bike into my walled garden around sundown,
they disappear. I never catch the exact moment.
When I go to bed I lodge a brick against the base of my door
so it doesn't swing open. I don't sleep well with that empty space
between me   and the girls behind the curtain.

Ghost Moon Lullaby

The children facing the cameras
don't complain. They're not fooled by concrete
or the lack of windows.
They know that borders mean nothing to ghosts
and that if they fall asleep under the moon
they'll wake up under a sun that will burn
the skin right off their flesh
leaving them with nothing but bones
not even a mother could recognize.
The guards don't understand
why they don't try to escape.

Shaping the Dark

I didn't know I was afraid of the dark
until it rose off blacktop and ran toward me
as if it had been waiting for me to round the corner
where the last streetlight burned a hole in the jungle night.

By the time I know the dark
is a dog, it's too late to turn.
All I can do is pedal faster and hope my fear
carries my bike past its teeth.

I could shout, but I don't. It's only when I realize
the dog is silent too, that I see it's
Chaparrita running toward me,
nipples swaying beneath her belly so swollen
it almost drags on the street. I brake,

flip down my kickstand,
get off and kneel before her.
When I press my face against her neck,
I breathe in hunger and dust and love.

Was she waiting for *me*?
It doesn't matter. I'm the one
who rode *toward* the dark sobbing her name:

  Chaparriiita!

How to See Light with Your Eyes Closed

When his fingers   open me   a seam of light   shines
in the dark earth.

I hold my breath   afraid   he won't see it   but his hand
    stills.

It is so dark   I can't see him   but when he speaks   the seam

swells.   I go down with it   on his words   meet his palm
with a moan

that is not an echo   but the ocean itself
as the moon   breaks   its silence.

Broken Water

When the deer
           lowered her head to drink
she was so lean
           I could see water ripple
under her fur.
           I wanted so much to stroke
the bridge of her nose, the bones of her face
                     under soft fur.
I wanted to lie with her
           in the goldenrod,
for her to teach me
           how to touch the earth
                with my whole body,
                     belly down,
as if I belonged to it.

           But she leaped into the brush
and I sank
        under the shadow of a dream
I didn't want, knowing thorns
would tear my skin if I followed.

I wanted so much—

        the source of tears—

to know if dreams began or ended with thirst.

Parting the Sea

I regret I didn't ask those girls
outside the bar next door
if I could have helped.
But what could I do?
Blades were real there,
not a metaphor for how we are most alive
when we stomp on death's edge
like a flamenco dancer
taunting the rabid dogs of destiny
that have chased her to the precipice.

43 students "disappeared" at Ayotzinapa,
most likely dead: suffocated, then burned,
ashes sent to a Swiss lab because nothing remained
that could be identified as human.

This is not the time to talk about the moon,
but I'm going to anyway, because the moon
rules the tides, and it's time to break the tyranny
of closed loops that keep those girls from walking away
and me from stopping to ask, "Can I help?"

Those aren't gunshots, Moon,
those are the black stilettos of a red-skirted dancer
stomping on your grave,
holding back the incoming tide so those lost girls
who lived right next to me
can make it to dry ground.

      With a flick of her wrist,
          waves crash
        subside into sea foam.

The disappeared   visible now

on the other side of a border
that can never be crossed   by men
who think they can control the force of water.

Left Without Words

The moon can't be understood
through butterflies or birdsong.
It's a man sliding his palm
down your belly saying
the most important thing is to feel loved
as he slips his fingers inside you,
stroking the places you were told to hide
before you could name them.
I lend you my body, says the Moon Man.
Then, when you hear these words,
when you *believe* them,
you'll understand the moon,
because to lend is not to give,
though at the time you'll think it is.

The Full Moon's Shadow

Beneath the fat pearl of a full moon
   strung on a strand of invisible stars,
     the withered Maya woman steps

into Tulum traffic
  as if the passing cars aren't real,
    walks past a restaurant where a girl

who should be singing to her ancestors
  turns away from the shining earth
    to watch a flat screen hung on a greasy wall.

This old woman,
  follows a path of glowing white shells
    no one else can see

to a temple where she will offer flowers
  at the wedding of a goddess to a god.
    She knows the light the screen emits

is not light,
  but it's shadow, what the light
    can't see about itself

  and must come to know on its own,
    too heavy
      for the stars to hold.

Mirror, Mirror

Moon, do you resent the sun?
Are you lonely? If I reach for you blind
across the footprints of the men
who thought by walking on you they owned you,
will you forgive yourself for being too beautiful?

What the Man in the Moon Has to Say

You say I'm cold, have no feelings.
You're the one that asked to shelter on my dark side.
Don't blame me for running out of oxygen.
Go stare at the sun if you want tears to relieve you.
I'm just a screen for rabbits and Swiss cheese
and Chinese cinnamon-peach princesses
and goofy men with smiles so wide you think
you are safe in a child's storybook when you're actually
perched on the lap of a pedophile.
I heard you sobbing last night.
I'll go on pulling water across Earth's surface
until it breaks and land is obliterated. I'm content
with my blank face. The one time I opened my eyes
I was blinded.

Breaking up with the Moon

I'm fed up with this soft-focus seduction
and your damn endless cycles
that keep me circling back to my wounds
when the sky in front of me is blue
and I'm surrounded by tropical greenery
and cheerful trilling birds.
At least they sound cheerful—
I realize I could be projecting.
They could be freaking out because
their nest is being invaded by a *terciopelo*,
the deadliest snake in the world.
But wouldn't they fly away?
Unless, *quelle horreur*—they're defending their eggs,
which I would say in Spanish
since that's the *lingua franca* in these parts,
but I don't know the equivalent words.
Ay caramba? Dios mio?
Maybe something like that,
but it doesn't really matter because—
news flash!—birds don't speak French or Spanish.
They speak bird, and not just one language.
There's hummingbird and vireo and woodpecker.
And not all hummingbirds, etc. speak one tongue.
Each species has a dialect with a name that's a poem.
Ruby-throated, broad-billed and violet-crowned,
calling out their own particular trills
so they can mate with their own kind
and not breed ruby-billed, broad-throated babies.

I don't know anything about bird language
besides that there are an awful lot of them
and that many are extinct, or will be soon,
like the ivory billed woodpecker,

known as the Lord God Bird because
that's what people cried out when they saw it.

Imagine how that last woodpecker felt
when it called and no one responded.

I'm so lonesome I could cry, Hank Williams sang,
the song Elvis said was the saddest he ever heard.
What's it like to know you're the last of your kind?
Is that when you stop flipping cottonmouths
out of the canoe? Is that when you let the gators
drag you under? Moon, I want to say
I want to see the world without shadows,
but it's not going to happen because
I can't hold time still. Instead of worrying about this,
instead of saying *whatever* or *why bother*,
I'm just going to break up with you.
On the movie screen of my mind
I'm going to stand in the street at high noon
and shoot the dead horses
of abandonment and betrayal in the balls.

You bet I'll flip that cottonmouth
and take that shot of *mezcal*.
If you want to pretend this is still a movie,
I can be redeemed and put the shot glass down,
but if you haven't figured out this is as deadly and real
as the *terciopelo* you're about to step on
there's not much hope for you.

Own it. I will. And I'll own those two glasses of wine
I had at dinner last Friday.
Dionysus, who am I to deny you? The sober say
it's a slippery slope. You, my juicy god reply,
would you want it to be anything else?

Poem to Our Third Body

You must have trusted us.
You must have been hungry   out there in the ether,
waiting for us on a steamy Mexican street
to cross paths over coffee
and conversation about angels
who longed so much for touch
they gave up their wings.

How our flavors when we kissed
must have burst on your tongue:
cilantro and saltwater,
chiles and espresso,
mangos so sticky and sweet our skin
was the feast the angels longed for.

We promised you a long life.
Poetry and kindness,
and long journeys into mountain valleys
to hear what waterfalls remembered
about the color of the sky
when the world was newborn.

I'm sorry we left you.

All I have for you are scraps of grief
I must throw to the dog now.
She still has muscle and bone. You are a ghost.
It's time you noticed.

Know you were loved
and please don't begrudge the dog her scraps.

I will have to die alone some day, too.

Thank you for going first.

Blessed without Words

The woman across the table is telling
the same story she told me in another Mexican town:
too many drinks, a lost phone,
a boyfriend back home who is too good for her.
After awhile, I'm just watching her lips move.
I imagine she's telling me a story I want to hear,
how the pit bulls imprisoned on Tulum's roof tops
leap off when the moon is full into puddles so deep
they can swallow a bike whole.

         A beggar
steps off the street, a cold knife
to cut Lorca's fruit, green and chilled.
He approaches our sidewalk table, slides
a paper slip in front of us both. My companion,
without looking up, says she'll have the mole enchiladas.
I'll be back, he motions when I look up,
moving on to the next table.
       While she talks
I translate to myself: *Hola, soy sordomudo.*
Hello, I am a deaf mute. *No puedo oir, no hablar.*
I can't hear or speak. *Ayudame por mis hijos
para poder comprarles utiles escolares.*
Help me buy school supplies for my children.
Ayudame de todo Corazon. Help me with all your heart.
Lo que usted guste. Whatever you like.

On the other side of the paper slip
the sign language alphabet and a sketch of the Virgin.
It's clear from the look on her face,
she's not questioning, like me,
why we have to suffer to know God's love.
She is beyond questions, while I panic

as the deaf mute circles back to our table.
The *pesos* in my pocket burn my thigh
with their cold heat. I hand them over.

     In a flash,
he is gone, absorbed by the shadows
past the awning's edge. The waiter steps forward,
back-lit by a corona of bare bulbs.
When he offers us menus
the shame that's been chasing this woman
from San Miguel de Allende to Tulum
steals her tongue. I order for us both:
dos jugos de piña y las enchiladas de mole.

She may have had too many drinks
in those other towns, but tonight she is sober.
I read the beggar's final words: *Dios bendiga su ayuda.*
This time I translate out loud. God bless your help.
Her hand shakes when she lifts the gold juice.
I take a sip myself.
    It is sweet
        going down.

My coins sob in the deaf mute's pocket
as they lose their chill.

Broken Chains

The deaf couple walks arm in arm
down the center of the unpaved road that ends
where the jungle begins.
They can't hear the underground water
pooling under the Yucatán,
but they see the dried-up puddles, skirt
the cracked mud without breaking contact.

The rooftop pit bulls rush to the edges,
barking their hell,
but the couple doesn't look up.
The spare change they begged off strangers
jingles like broken chains in their pockets.

Moon, what can I say besides
I'm sorry you're not free, too?

You must go on pulling the tide
in and out. You must keep shining
so lovers can look at each other without
running from each others' wounds.

Let it be enough that he and I tried to open our eyes
wide enough to see beyond our reflections.

The light is broken, but the chains are, too.
The last I heard of the deaf couple
they were walking arm in arm,
motioning a story to each other
we'll never know.

In Ceremony

When the guitar penetrated the dark
the girl next to me began to weep.
I wanted to crawl across the earth floor
and take her to my heart,
coax her back against the clay wall
until she felt the mountain
beating beneath us,
but I was too afraid of my own shame
to touch her. I knew she needed to cry

without comfort
until there were no tears left for herself.
Then she could walk out into the morning
to see the hummingbird
                      drop from the sun,

wings heard, but not seen,

seed syllables
whirling down the mountain
to gild the open flowers with stardust.

Confessional

There is no past tense
for falling water
and no way to go back:
only round. Clouds swell
and let go of edges
they aren't aware of,
waterfalls bomb down gulches
funneled by flat land
that gives way to get
what it wants, slowing
the water with its curves
to feed roots
so trees can lift their leaves
to the clouds. If the river
ends in the ocean
it's impossible to say
where a raindrop goes,
but I still want to say it,
as if syllables could absolve me
from what came after
I took off my clothes at the waterfall.
I don't want to need you
to witness my shame any more.
The river has overflowed
its banks many times
since I stepped in.
Please accept this gardenia
opening to the rain
whose scent saw me through
afternoons I believed
it would never stop falling.

Breathing Again after a Long Time Underwater

Reaching my hands
into the late afternoon light
glowing on the river's final curve,
I didn't believe I was beautiful,
like the valley's wild horses that hid in high ferns
I parted like lace curtains with my hands,
a swimmer moving through water that closed behind me
without a ripple.

I came to a clearing. Light streamed down
to gild the filigreed edges where I stood
watching a wild mare on the far side watch me
with the wide, liquid eyes of one
who can see in the dark without stumbling
as her foal, still coated in its slick caul,
rose on shaky legs, then collapsed in birth blood.
For a few moments I forgot I was a human
who could kill what I should love.

At dusk I bathed at the river's edge
where the horses came out of the ferns,
moving silently over fallen needles
toward the breaking ocean.
Sharks waited there for offal to wash down—
pig carcasses, jaws hacked out by hunters to mount.

People disappeared all the time in that valley.
I was just a girl at the edge of a clearing.

I don't need to tell the story of how I was
broken anymore. Now I can speak
of how a wild horse watched me from the ironwoods
and of how warm the river was
when I knelt to lift the late afternoon light
out of the water.

How I poured it over my head.
How it flowed down my hair and shoulders,
gilding my skin, returned to the river unbroken.

That Which There Are No Words For
—In memoriam, Sandy Hook, Dec. 14, 2012

All afternoon on the oyster farm
a great egret watched me work
hoisting bags of oysters
out of the shallow water
onto the dock to sort.

It was dark of the moon, tide lower
than I'd ever seen it, exposing rocks,
a pile of culch I'd dumped at the edge of the marsh,
mud speckled with dead slipper shells,
crabs that could be hibernating.

Oysters, sealed tight, holding
their mouthful of saltwater in deep cups
polished smooth inside by flesh,
passed through my gloved fingers,
sorting for market.

I wasn't thinking about thresholds,
how often we cross without knowing,
doors opening and closing
without a creak or click as the latch catches
and we wonder what side we are on now.

My body had taken over: bend, hoist,
dump, sort, back into the old bag
to grow another winter underwater,
or into a wider mesh
strung on a line close to shore for market.

I broke apart the fused ones,
pulled the beards off mussels
and tossed them overboard,
rescued small crabs who clung or froze,
imagining then I couldn't see them.

Minnows thrashed in my palms,
a surge of pure light and muscle.
When I released them back to the muddy water
through my cold fingers
joy flashed like quicksilver.

I wasn't thinking about thresholds,
I was on my hands and knees
pushing oyster bags through six inches of water,
sucked down when I tried to stand,
forced to crawl, cursing and laughing

as the egret, who had not moved in hours,
took a few elegant steps, rippling the calm.

Sitting up, kneeling in my waders,
waist-deep in mud,
I closed my eyes,
not because I knew what was coming,
but to see in the dark as well.

The white feathers of the egret so fine and smooth.
The marsh, golden in mid-December.

It was the day before our darkness made itself known,
that which we'd say about after,
There were no words for.
Crow call in the east answered by one at my back,
Prepare to be emptied.

The death of innocence is one way to learn
how to love. In the dark, I pray for another,
pure as white feathers, a breath
passing with ease through my body,
turned to the low sun moving across the marsh.

Where the Sky Is Born

When we enter the water he says
I am to trust and surrender.
He will move my body. I am to let go.

The clay laguna bottom is white as the moon,
nothing between it and the sun
                but a few feet of water so blue...

(I want to trust again the whisper and lap my rising blood.)

We stop when the water is waist high.
My eyes are level with his heart.
He watches me like a heron
who can stand on one leg for hours.
We are so still tiny translucent fish
eat the dead skin off our submerged legs,
disappear in a flash of silver when I skim
the surface with my fingertips
drawing a circle around us that ripples out
to the waiting shore.

(I am to trust and surrender. He will move my body.
                                   I am to let go.)

I float on my back, close my eyes to the sun.
He cradles my head like a newborn's
until I give my weight to the water,
rolls me over and down, holding me under past the fear
I'll never breathe again
                until I forget I will need to.

When he lifts me to the surface I
exhale first, then inhale. Skin sliding over bones,

I breathe my way back to where the sky is born.

It doesn't matter he is not my lover.
I lay in the shallows and he cups my closed eyes
so when I open them I'm not blinded.

Blue butterflies   vibrate   in the air between us.

The ancient sadness in his eyes draws my gaze skyward—
two white cranes   cross wings   then disappear
            into the sun.

Jennifer Lighty's work has been lauded by the Rhode Island State Council on the Arts, nominated for The Pushcart Prize, Best New Poets, and been published in *The Beloit Poetry Journal, Verse Daily, Thrush Poetry Journal, Earthlines, The Island Review, The North American Review, Poet Lore, Off The Coast, Room, Bamboo Ridge, Cutthroat* and many other journals. For over 20 years she lived on Block Island, a small island off the Rhode Island coast where she learned to listen to wind, waves, birdsong, deer tracks and silence. While living there she was a part of The Block Island Poetry Project, a creative community that inspires regular folks to sing, dance, and write from their souls. While there, she taught a series of innovative workshops grounded in permaculture, deep ecology and archetypal psychology that combined writing, movement, meditation and getting outdoors that developed into a popular online workshop, "The 30 Day Poetry Challenge." She is the author of *Weaving a Basket of Words: How To Write a Poem That Will Carry Water*, an online book that helps writers develop craft as well as creativity. 8 years ago she began to travel and has spent significant amounts of time in Peru, Mexico, Hawaii and Central America. Recently, she became a janzu massage therapist and will be sharing this water rebirthing practice on Maui and worldwide. www.songofthebutterfly.co waveofchange@gmail.com

www.ingramcontent.com/pod-product-compliance
Lightning Source LLC
Chambersburg PA
CBHW060225050426
42446CB00013B/3175